CW00686973

Who is my neighbour? In Luke's Gospel, was 'anxious to justify himself' (Luke 10: love. Christ's response, which took the f Samaritan, is interesting for its lack of pr say about what it is to be a good neighb neighbour might be too closely. All we know of the man the Good Sam... helped is that he was on his way from Jerusalem to Jericho. In other words the neighbour to be loved is anybody who presents themselves.

Who is my Neighbour? is an opportunity to reflect on the lawyer's question. In the past responding to this question may have been relatively easy. Individual circumstances aside, neighbours tended to be much like each other. Today, society is more diverse and less homogenous. Our experience at home, at work and in our parishes calls forth a different response. My neighbour is not necessarily a person whose language, culture or experience I can immediately identify with.

It is nearly two years since I outlined my pastoral priorities for the Diocese of Westminster. Running through these is a concern for *communio*; for the building up of vibrant parishes where there is a real sense of belonging. It is for this reason that I have placed such an emphasis on the small faith sharing groups who will be using this booklet. Central to *communio* is an awareness of others. How easy it is to go to church Sunday after Sunday with little regard to those who gather with us? Equally compelling, is the question of how newcomers are received. St. Paul reminded us that in Christ there can be no Jew or Greek, slave or free and so it must be in our communities. Where society sees a 'foreigner' or a 'stranger' we are called to see a brother and sister in the Lord. How we receive others, will say a lot about the nature and strength of our communities. Where a community does not welcome those who present themselves, how can it reach out to those who do not? This Lent may we take to heart the words of St. Paul. 'Welcome one another, therefore, just as Christ has welcomed you, for the glory of God' (Romans 15: 7).

With my blessing and prayers,

+ Cormac Murphy-O'Connor

Cardinal Cormac Murphy-O'Connor
Archbishop of Westminster

Who is my neighbour? is an opportunity to reflect on our welcome and understanding of others in our parishes. Running over six weeks, *Who is my neighbour?* includes six sessions for small groups or communities, as well as a series of daily meditations which you may wish to use on your own. The booklet reflects on the quality of welcome a newcomer might receive, asking whether or not we have taken the trouble to discover something of their story, address their needs, recognise their giftedness and be reshaped by their presence.

Group Reflections

These begin with an opening prayer drawing on the psalms and a few moments of silence. The opening prayer is followed by a Scripture passage and a reflection. Following each of these there is an opportunity for the group to share their thoughts and to explore the implications for Christian living. This period of reflection and sharing can be drawn to a close using the excerpt from *Erga migrantes caritas Christi* (The love of Christ towards Migrants), a document from the Pontifical Council for the Pastoral Care of Migrants and Itinerant People (May 2004). The session is concluded with a series of petitions and a closing prayer.

Daily Meditations

The daily meditations for Sundays provide a background to the Scriptural passage used in the group sessions and are drawn from the Sunday readings. Mondays, Wednesdays and Fridays also draw on the Scripture from the previous Sunday. To help our preparation for the Sunday Mass the Saturday meditation will use the Gospel passage to be used the next day. On Tuesdays and Thursdays the daily meditations will take the form of a testimony. These testimonies were either written specially for this booklet or were taken from *The Ground of Justice*, a report commissioned by the Dioceses of Brentwood, Southwark and Westminster. Holy Week follows a similar pattern but without the use of testimonies.

Church documents & Texts

A number of Church documents are referred to in the course of this booklet. You may wish to explore the following further: *Lumen Gentium*, the Second Vatican Council's Dogmatic Constitution on the Church (November 1964). *Gaudium et Spes* is the Second Vatican Council's Pastoral Constitution on the Church in the Modern World (December 1965). References are also made to Pope John Paul II's documents *Veritatis Splendor* – on the Church's moral teaching (August 1993); *Evangelium Vitae* - on the Value and Inviolability of Human Life (March 1995); *Centesimus Annus* – letter on 100th anniversary of Leo XIII's encyclical on Capital and Labour, *Rerum Novarum* (May, 1991); *Familiaris Consortio* – on the role of the Christian Family (November 1981) and *Novo Millennio ineunte* - letter at the close of the Jubilee Year 2000 (January 2001). These documents can all be found on the Vatican website (www.vatican.va).

Opening Prayer

Leader: O come, let us sing to the Lord
let us make a joyful noise to the rock of our salvation!
Let us come into his presence with thanksgiving;
let us make a joyful noise to him with songs of praise!

Group: **For the Lord is a great God,**
and a great King above all gods.
In his hand are the depths of the earth;
the heights of the mountains are his also.
The sea is his, for he made it,
and the dry land, which his hands have formed.

Leader: O come, let us worship and bow down,
let us kneel before the Lord, our Maker!
For he is our God, and we are the people of his pasture,
and the sheep of his hand.

From Psalm 95

All: **Glory be to the Father...**

Leader: Lord, in this moment of silence
help us to be still
so that your word may enter our minds,
touch our hearts,
and direct our lives to you.

After a short silence the group or an individual says:

Gracious and holy Father,
give us wisdom to perceive you,
intelligence to understand you,
diligence to seek you,
patience to wait for you,
eyes to behold you,
a heart to meditate on you,
and a life to proclaim you;
through the power of the
Spirit of Jesus Christ our Lord,
Amen.

St. Benedict of Nursia (c.480-c.547)

**Explore the Sunday Scriptures for the First Sunday of Lent
(Genesis 2:7-9, 3:1-7)**

The Lord God fashioned man of dust from the soil. Then he breathed into his nostrils a breath of life, and thus man became a living being.

The Lord God planted a garden in Eden which is in the east, and there he put the man he had fashioned. The Lord God caused to spring up from the soil every kind of tree, enticing to look at and good to eat, with the tree of life and the tree of the knowledge of good and evil in the middle of the garden.

The serpent was the most subtle of all the wild beasts that the Lord God had made. It asked the woman, 'Did God really say you were not to eat from any of the trees in the garden?' The woman answered the serpent, 'We may eat the fruit of the trees in the garden. But of the fruit of the tree in the middle of the garden God said, "You must not eat it, nor touch it, under pain of death." ' Then the serpent said to the woman, 'No! You will not die! God knows in fact that on the day you eat it your eyes will be opened and you will be like gods, knowing good and evil.' The woman saw that the tree was good to eat and pleasing to the eye, and that it was desirable for the knowledge that it could give. So she took some of its fruit and ate it. She gave some also to her husband who was with her, and he ate it. Then the eyes of both of them were opened and they realised that they were naked. So they sewed fig-leaves together to make themselves loin-cloths.

Following a short period of silence you may wish to share an image, a thought, a phrase, a question that has struck you.

For Reflection

Before we are European, American, Australasian, African or Asian we have a common beginning in God. It was he who breathed the breath of life into each of us. Moreover, having gifted us with life, God created everything that is necessary for living. At the same time he conferred upon us the greatest of dignities: the freedom to love him or reject him. Time and again we forget all of this. We question God in the face of famine, as if the scarcity of resources that leads to want has nothing to do with our inability to distribute these resources fairly. Similarly, in the face of war and conflict, it is easy to pass over the fact that violence is somebody's abuse of the free choice God has generously given. And then, when faced with a 'stranger', especially somebody of a different race, culture or background to our own, we can forget that the things which divide people from each other, and from God, are of our own making.

Christ came to heal the sin and division that marks our lives. In baptism, we became one with Christ and thus, we became sons and daughters of God, our Father. In other words, we became brothers and sisters not only of Jesus but also of each other.

Whatever our nationality we are members of the family of God. In the Church, words like 'stranger' and 'foreigner' seem rather inappropriate. Indeed there is only one banquet and one host; each of us, no matter who, is a guest of the one Lord.

In the story of creation Adam and Eve were enticed by the thought that they would be like gods. Immersed in the material world and striving for position and status, we can be similarly enticed. Just as Adam and Eve failed to contemplate the consequences of their actions, how often do we fail to reflect on the bigger picture? How often, in relation to the world in which we live, and in relation to others, of whatever race, creed and colour, do we want to be gods – almighty and all powerful?

Share your thoughts on this reflection. How does this week's Scripture reading and reflection encourage you? Where are you affirmed? Where are you challenged? What impact might this have on your daily living?

From Erga migrantes caritas Christi (The love of Christ towards migrants)

22 Welcoming the stranger… remains a permanent feature of the Church of God. It is practically marked by the vocation to be in exile, in diaspora, dispersed among cultures and ethnic groups without ever identifying itself completely with any of these. Otherwise it would cease to be the first-fruit and sign, the leaven and prophecy of the universal Kingdom and community that welcomes every human being without preference for persons or peoples. Welcoming the stranger is…intrinsic to the nature of the Church itself and bears witness to its fidelity to the gospel.

Leader: Aloud or in the silence of our hearts let us bring to the Father our thanks (pause)…

Leader: In sorrow let us ask the Father for forgiveness (pause)…

Leader: With confidence let us entrust to the Father our cares and concerns (pause)…

Closing Prayer

Lord, forgive us the times we have ignored those in need,
or refused a welcome to those you have embraced.
Strengthen us with your grace, open our hearts,
that our thoughts, words and deeds,
may reflect your love for the neighbours you set before us,
for you live and reign with the Father and the Holy Spirit,
one God, for ever and ever.
Amen.

Who is My Neighbour?

My neighbour has been created by God.
My neighbour is precious in God's sight.
My neighbour is equally entitled to the earth's resources.
My neighbour is someone to be embraced.

Read the Scripture from the First Sunday of Lent (Year A) - Genesis 2:7-9, 3:1-7

The version used at Mass can be found at the beginning of the Group Session for Week One (p. 7-8). You may, of course, read from your own Bible.

Background

In this text (the Greek term Genesis means origin) the priestly editors have retained an older form (from their own material in Genesis 1:1-2:4a) of the tradition relating to the creation of humanity and the entry into the world of human disobedience to the will of God. This ancient text argues that man emerged from the earth and that God imparted to him creative energy (Genesis 2:7). Eden is considered as paradise believed to be an oasis in the Mesopotamian desert (1 Chronicles 1:9) where this creative energy might be lived in primal innocence. By creating the serpent (in Hebrew a word-play on 'subtle' and 'naked') God is testing the man (Adam) and woman (Eve) in order to determine the extent of their obedience to God's will in this paradisal context. They fail the test by agreeing to the serpent's suggestion to consume the forbidden fruit. As a result of eating the fruit their disobedience placed them both at variance with God's plan for humanity and elevated them (as 'gods', Genesis 3:5) to a divine status. This action, ironically, enables them to distinguish the difference between good and evil. Through this narrative the priestly editors believed that they had explained to the community the origin both of life and sinfulness.

O Lord my God,
teach my heart this day where and how to see You,
where and how to find You.
Let me seek You in my desire,
let me desire You in my seeking.
Let me find You by loving You,
let me love You when I find You.
Amen.   *St. Anselm of Canterbury (1033-1109)*

dust from the soil

Each year, on Ash Wednesday, we come forward to receive ashes. With ash on his thumb, the priest traces the Sign of the Cross on our foreheads saying the words: 'Remember, (wo)man, that you are dust and to dust you will return.' We are reminded of God's magnificent work of creation. Most importantly though, we are reminded of Christ's death on the Cross, by which we are offered the promise of eternal life - a powerful thought to contemplate as we begin our Lenten journey.

As we get on with our day, we often come across others with a smudge of ash on their foreheads either in the workplace, on local transport or in our local shops. Often, that smudge 'breaks the ice' and we set aside the idea that it is strictly a private matter to acknowledge our faith even to a complete stranger. We sense a connection - because we are connected through our baptism - and quite often extend a greeting. Although ashes are only distributed annually, we are regularly reminded of our baptismal connections in the celebration of the Eucharist. Perhaps, we could extend a greeting to a complete stranger more often - just as Jesus would have done on his earthly journeys.

From Lumen Gentium (Christ, Light of Nations)

9. At all times and in every race God has given welcome to whosoever fears Him and does what is right. God, however, does not make men holy and save them merely as individuals, without bond or link between one another. Rather has it pleased Him to bring men together as one people, a people which acknowledges Him in truth and serves Him in holiness.

O Lord my God,
teach my heart this day where and how to see You,
where and how to find You.
Let me seek You in my desire,
let me desire You in my seeking.
Let me find You by loving You,
let me love You when I find You.
Amen.

St. Anselm of Canterbury (1033-1109)

Marcos arrived in the UK in April 2005. Before that he had been working for the Brazilian government and as a taxi driver. However, shortly before coming to Britain he lost his job. At his age finding a new job in Brazil was not easy, more so as the country's economy was not flourishing. His friend, who was already working in the UK, suggested he try his luck here, promised to help him find a job and bought him a plane ticket. After arriving in England, Marcos had three stressful months, while trying to find a simple, low paid job. In addition to his age, one of the difficulties the fact that he did not speak English. Meanwhile his friend was covered all his expenses.

Marcos, 50, Brazilian taken from *The Ground of Justice*

From Erga migrantes caritas Christi

9. Migration imposes new commitments of evangelisation and solidarity on Christians and calls them to examine more profoundly those values shared by other religious or lay groups… This new historical context is characterised by the thousand different faces of humanity and, unlike the past, diversity is becoming commonplace in many countries. Therefore Christians are called to give witness to and practise not only the spirit of tolerance… but also respect for the other's identity.

O Lord my God,
teach my heart this day where and how to see You,
where and how to find You.
Let me seek You in my desire,
let me desire You in my seeking.
Let me find You by loving You,
let me love You when I find You.
Amen.

St. Anselm of Canterbury (1033-1109)

knowledge of good and evil

Parents, regardless of what religion they practise or even if it is none at all, generally expend considerable time and energy helping their children to discern good and evil. However, given that society today seems to define conscience as essentially a matter of personal preference, the task can seem quite daunting. Yet, in addition to the gifts of intellect and free will that our loving Father bestowed on humankind, he offered the commandments to help us frame our Christian conscience. While negative precepts may immediately spring to mind, it is important to remember that through his earthly ministry, Jesus gave us positive direction – reminding us that self-giving is the key to growing closer to God. Referring to Christ's teaching of the two commandments of love of God and love of neighbour in his encyclical, *Veritatis Splendor* (The Splendour of Truth) Pope John Paul II explained that the commandments must not be viewed as 'minimum limits' but 'lofty challenges' for 'a loving heart'. 'Thus, the commandment "You shall not murder" becomes a call to an attentive love which protects and promotes the life of one's neighbour' (VS, 15).

From Veritatis Splendor (The Splendour of Truth)

14. Both the Old and New Testaments explicitly affirm that without love of neighbour, made concrete in keeping the commandments, genuine love of God is not possible.

O Lord my God,
teach my heart this day where and how to see You,
where and how to find You.
Let me seek You in my desire,
let me desire You in my seeking.
Let me find You by loving You,
let me love You when I find You.
Amen.

St. Anselm of Canterbury (1033-1109)

'It is not good for man to be alone'

I go to the Mass to pray with the Catholic community, to develop my relationship with Jesus Christ and to interact with the members of the community. My experiences in Ethiopia and Britain have been very different.

In Ethiopia there is a lot of interaction. At church, people greet and talk to each other, sharing their feelings openly, showing love to each other, helping and cheering up needy individuals and those who are alone. Visiting the sick and inviting people home for a meal or coffee are common practices. There is always someone to turn to in a time of need. I find a real sense of happiness and hope. In Britain things are very different. People seem more distanced from each other, even lonely. Before and after Mass they don't seem to greet and talk to each other in the same way.

Going to church is so much more than attending a ceremony and then going home. It is a time for us to get to know each other, to support each other, to bring into each other's lives the love of Christ which we have celebrated and received at Mass.

Bersisa (Ethiopia)

O Lord my God,
teach my heart this day where and how to see You,
where and how to find You.
Let me seek You in my desire,
let me desire You in my seeking.
Let me find You by loving You,
let me love You when I find You.
Amen.

St. Anselm of Canterbury (1033-1109)

they were naked

When Adam and Eve realised they were naked, they tried to cover themselves, to hide from God. They were ashamed. Shame remains prevalent today, in particular, for those in new situations and new surroundings. Feelings of inferiority can easily arise as people are embarrassed by their inability to communicate in a new language, to afford fashionable clothes or to easily adjust easily to local customs.

In his seminal work on the theology of the body, Pope John Paul II wrote extensively about Adam and Eve's original state of nakedness prior to the visit from the serpent. He explained that they inwardly shared the vision of their Creator, that 'everything [God] had made... was very good.' (Genesis 1:31). Sadly, their eyes were not opened by the forbidden fruit but instead they became blinded by vice - vanity, greed and envy.

Just as our loving Father sees beyond the fig leaves, Christ saw more than tax collectors and lepers among the outcasts who he encountered in his travels. We too are invited to see beyond the surface - to see the good in our neighbour and to remember that each person regardless of race or nationality is made in the image and likeness of God.

From Gaudium et Spes (Joy and hope)

12. For Sacred Scripture teaches that man was created 'to the image of God' as able to know and love his creator, and as set by him over all earthly creatures that he might rule them and make use of them, while glorifying God.

O Lord my God,
teach my heart this day where and how to see You,
where and how to find You.
Let me seek You in my desire,
let me desire You in my seeking.
Let me find You by loving You,
let me love You when I find You.
Amen.

St. Anselm of Canterbury (1033-1109)

Six days later, Jesus took with him Peter and James and his brother John and led them up a high mountain where they could be alone. There in their presence he was transfigured; his face shone like the sun and his clothes became as white as the light. Suddenly Moses and Elijah appeared to them; they were talking with him. Then Peter spoke to Jesus. 'Lord,' he said 'it is wonderful for us to be here; if you wish, I will make three tents here, one for you, one for Moses and one for Elijah.' He was still speaking when suddenly a bright cloud covered them with shadow, and from the cloud there came a voice which said, 'This is my Son, the Beloved; he enjoys my favour. Listen to him.' When they heard this, the disciples fell on their faces, overcome with fear. But Jesus came up and touched them. 'Stand up,' he said 'do not be afraid.' And when they raised their eyes they saw no one but only Jesus.

As they came down from the mountain Jesus gave them this order, 'Tell no one about the vision until the Son of Man has risen from the dead.'

Matthew 17:1-9

When have we tried to hold on to a situation, to preserve the status quo? When have we been open to God, trusting in his judgement and loving plan?

O Lord my God,
teach my heart this day where and how to see You,
where and how to find You.
Let me seek You in my desire,
let me desire You in my seeking.
Let me find You by loving You,
let me love You when I find You.
Amen.

St. Anselm of Canterbury (1033-1109)

Opening Prayer

Leader:

God is our refuge and strength,
a very present help in trouble.

Group:

Therefore we will not fear,
though the earth should change,
though the mountains shake in the heart of the sea;
though its waters roar and foam,
though the mountains tremble with its tumult.

Leader:

There is a river whose streams
make glad the city of God,
the holy habitation of the Most High.
God is in the midst of the city;
it shall not be moved;
God will help it when the morning dawns.

From Psalm 46

All:

Glory be to the Father...

Leader:

Lord, in this moment of silence
help us to be still
so that your word may enter our minds,
touch our hearts,
and direct our lives to you.

After a short silence the group or an individual says:

Gracious and holy Father,
give us wisdom to perceive you,
intelligence to understand you,
diligence to seek you,
patience to wait for you,
eyes to behold you,
a heart to meditate on you,
and a life to proclaim you;
through the power of the
Spirit of Jesus Christ our Lord,
Amen.

St. Benedict of Nursia (c.480-c.547)

Explore the Sunday Scriptures for the Second Sunday of Lent (Genesis 12:1-4)

The Lord said to Abram, 'Leave your country, your family and your father's house, for the land I will show you. I will make you a great nation; I will bless you and make your name so famous that it will be used as a blessing.

'I will bless those who bless you: I will curse those who slight you. All the tribes of the earth shall bless themselves by you.'

So Abram went as the Lord told him.

Following a short period of silence you may wish to share an image, a thought, a phrase, a question that has struck you.

For Reflection

Abram, later renamed Abraham, was a man of great faith. In fact, it is his faith that the world's three major religions, Judaism, Christianity and Islam look to. Because he was a man of faith Abram trusted in the promises that the Lord made him and left his homeland for another place. It is easy from the comfort of one's own home and culture to make all sorts of assumptions about why the 'foreigner' has often come to live among us. For the refugee, being here is not the result of a freely made decision. Moreover, even where the decision has been freely made, the leaving of country, family and father's house often leaves the newcomer in a particularly vulnerable position. What can it be to establish yourself in another country or to build a home and raise a young family without that support which the wider family so often offers? How easy or fulfilling is it to work where you do not know the language, where your presence may be resented, and your skills and achievements go unrecognised? For the migrant, as for anyone, the 'Promised Land' can seem a long way off. Away from country, friends and family, in what can be a fairly hostile environment, the only constant in a migrant's life, the only familiar territory that the migrant can bring with them, is his or her faith. How important then the welcome that he or she receives from the community of faith! How important the liturgy, prayer and devotions that have fed their faith.

How many are newcomers? How many of 'us' are children of migrants? Consider the congregation that gathers around you on Sunday. Look also at your colleagues or the people you pass on the way to work. What sacrifices have they had to make? What prejudices have they encountered? What roots have they had to put down? What transitions have they lived through? What act of faith have they had to make?

Share your thoughts on this reflection. How does this week's Scripture reading and reflection encourage you? Where are you affirmed? Where are you challenged? What impact might this have on your daily living?

From Erga migrantes caritas Christi

13. This vision leads us to approach migration in the light of those biblical events that mark the phases of humanity's arduous journey towards the birth of a people without discrimination or frontiers, depository of God's gift for all nations and open to man's eternal vocation. Faith perceives in it the journey of the Patriarchs, sustained by the promise as they moved towards the future homeland, and that of the Hebrews, freed from slavery, as they crossed the Red Sea in the Exodus, that formed the People of the Covenant. Again, in a certain sense, faith finds in migration an exile, in which every goal reached in fact is relative. In migration faith discovers once more the universal message of the prophets, who denounce discrimination, oppression, deportation, dispersion and persecution as contrary to God's plan. At the same time they proclaim salvation for all, witnessing even in the chaotic events and contradictions of human history, that God continues to work out his plan of salvation until all things are brought together in Christ (cf. Ephesians 1:10).

Leader: Aloud or in the silence of our hearts let us bring to the Father our thanks (pause)…

Leader: In sorrow let us ask the Father for forgiveness (pause)…

Leader: With confidence let us entrust to the Father our cares and concerns (pause)…

Closing Prayer

Lord, forgive us the times we have ignored those in need,
or refused a welcome to those you have embraced.
Strengthen us with your grace, open our hearts,
that our thoughts, words and deeds,
may reflect your love for the neighbours you set before us,
for you live and reign with the Father and the Holy Spirit,
one God, for ever and ever.
Amen.

Who is My Neighbour?

My neighbour may be in exile.
My neighbour may have left country, family and home.
My neighbour's need may be greater than mine.
My neighbour has surmounted hurdles I can only imagine.

Read the Scripture from the Second Sunday of Lent (Year A) - Genesis 12:1-4

The version used at Mass can be found at the beginning of the Group Session for Week Two (p.21). You may, of course, read from your own Bible.

Background

Abraham is considered to be the father of three faiths: Judaism, Christianity and Islam. In this text we are presented with the origin of the Abrahamic faith. In Genesis 17:5 Abram's name (exalted father) is changed to Abraham (father of nations) to mark his new status as a 'minister' of God's covenant which is entered through the rite of circumcision (Genesis 17:11). The narrative relating to Abram begins at Genesis 11:26 with a description of his family and their origin in Ur of the Chaldees, an ancient city of Mesopotamia (present day Iraq. Today, many Iraqi Christians are having to leave that area in search of peace and stability. Let us keep them in our prayers and offer our support where needed). Genesis 11:26 reveals Israel's origin among the Mesopotamian nations and of the nomadic existence of Abram and his clan who journey from Ur to the city of Haran at the source of the river Euphrates.

In Genesis 12:1 Abram becomes a 'pilgrim' as a result of obeying the call of 'the Lord' (Hebrew - Yahweh). Abram departs Haran for Canaan (Genesis 12:5). He receives from Yahweh the promise of a seven-fold blessing. This blessing is concentrated on Abram's role in being Yahweh's instrument through which all the nations will be blessed. Unlike the primal man and woman, Abram is portrayed as one who acted in obedience to God's will (Genesis 12:4a). As a result of Abram's faith Israel is granted the possibility of becoming the centre of universal solidarity for all nations (see also Isaiah 2:2 and Micah 4:2).

Make us worthy, Lord,
to serve those throughout the world
who live and die in poverty and hunger.
Give them through our hands,
this day their daily bread,
and by our understanding love, give peace and joy.
Amen.

Pope Paul VI (1897-1978)

your name

The fabric of family life is woven with stories. Young children never tire of hearing the story of how their parents decided on their particular name. Similarly, adults often look back fondly on the story behind their naming, as it brings to mind a relative (perhaps with some eccentric habits) or a family friend who has gone before us. There is a sense of connection.

Those who practice the Jewish faith, have long celebrated ceremonies in which the name of their newborn is announced. In baptism, the Christian receives his or her name in the Church. It is at that time that we become one with Christ and connected to the parish community. While this name gives a person their individual identity among friends and family, it also places them within the family of the Church. How often do we look around the parish community and wonder just who these people are – their names and where they are from? How often have we used names or labels abusing and patronising others? Just as God calls each of us by name, giving us value and affording us dignity, we too are invited to extend a greeting and to do the same to those around us.

From the Compendium of the Catechism

358. What is the root of human dignity? The dignity of the human person is rooted in his or her creation in the image and likeness of God. Endowed with a spiritual and immortal soul, intelligence and free will, the human person is ordered to God and called in soul and in body to eternal beatitude.

Make us worthy, Lord,
to serve those throughout the world
who live and die in poverty and hunger.
Give them through our hands,
this day their daily bread,
and by our understanding love, give peace and joy.
Amen.   *Pope Paul VI (1897-1978)*

My name is Teuta.

Teuta, my parents said, was the first Queen of the Illyrian tribe from which Albanians descended. Therefore, there is some strength and dignity by my name, but my true strength and dignity have always been in the love that Jesus has shown to me throughout my life.

I come from Albania, a tiny country which was under strict communist rule after WWII. Our borders were closed; the churches and mosques were destroyed; and even private practice of religion was not allowed. I had to keep silent outside about what went on at home. One day, at nursery, I almost destroyed my parents' lives when my teacher asked me to recite a little poem. Well, the only poems I knew were 'Hail Mary, full of grace…' and 'Our Father, who art in heaven…'. They would have gone to prison if I had opened my mouth. So I shrugged my shoulders and my teacher said that I should be ashamed not to know any poetry about our Mother – The Labour Party – and our Father – Comrade Enver Hoxha.

I remember standing in front of a map of the world where I had drawn a little cross as a blessing for my country just under where it said – Albania, but because it is such a tiny country, my cross seemed to be swimming over the Mediterranean Sea. That was to be the night when I would really set off by sea without saying goodbye to my land and to the people I loved, especially my grandmother. I still remember the difficult journey we had in detail. But it is not a unique journey. I know many people pass through similar experiences to get to a safer place. Many know the horrors of being in an over-crowded boat that has got far too much weight as the threatening waves keep jumping on top of you. Many know the long silence and darkness of the back of a lorry, but I do not know how I would have gone through it all without my mother's hand and our silent prayers.

My childhood home in Albania is still so vivid. I long for the smell of home; the sound of the Drini river passing by; the people whose dry-skinned wrinkles only accentuated their smiles... But, it had to end. It's the will of God and he has now blessed me with a lot of people and things that I would have never known. We can go to church now and at Easter, I don't have to eat the red eggs in hiding.

I am Teuta from Albania and this is my story.

Teuta is a character based on the experience of many Albanian migrants

Make us worthy, Lord,
to serve those throughout the world
who live and die in poverty and hunger.
Give them through our hands,
this day their daily bread,
and by our understanding love, give peace and joy.
Amen.

Pope Paul VI (1897-1978)

A blessing…

'A blessing to one another', a highly acclaimed exhibit touring America, highlights John Paul II's contribution to the strengthening of relations between Christians and Jews. It takes its name from the Pope's appeal marking the 50th anniversary of the 1943 Warsaw Ghetto uprising: 'As Christians and Jews, following the example of the faith of Abraham, we are called to be a blessing to the world. This is a common task awaiting us. It is therefore necessary for us, Christians and Jews, to first be a blessing to one another.'

Jesus walked from town to town through Judea, Galilee and Samaria meeting and ministering to those in need. This 'common task', to be a blessing to one another extends to all humankind as we are called to live our faith, imitating Jesus' actions through acts of love and charity.

From Evangelium Vitae (The Gospel of Life)

87. In our service of charity, we must be inspired and distinguished by a specific attitude: we must care for the other as a person for whom God has made us responsible. As disciples of Jesus, we are called to become neighbours of everyone (cf. Luke 10:29-37), and to show special favour to those who are poorest, most alone and most in need. In helping the hungry, the thirsty, the foreigner, the naked, the sick, the imprisoned – as well as the child in the womb and the old person who is suffering or near death – we have the opportunity to serve Jesus.

Make us worthy, Lord,
to serve those throughout the world
who live and die in poverty and hunger.
Give them through our hands,
this day their daily bread,
and by our understanding love, give peace and joy.
Amen.

Pope Paul VI (1897-1978)

'I didn't want to leave Poland. But at the same time I knew I could never do there what I really wanted to do. My big passion was to coach kids in ice-skating and I did it for some time. But it took three months to get paid and I don't even want to say how much it was... Then I told myself, "wake up, how are you going to survive?" So I was crying when I was leaving Poland but I didn't expect my parents to support me when I was 27 years old.'

Polish woman taken from *The Ground of Justice*

From Erga migrantes caritas Christi

36. Keeping our eyes on the gospel... means attention to people too, to their dignity and freedom. Helping them advance integrally requires a commitment to fraternity, solidarity, service and justice. The love of God, while it gives humankind the truth and shows everyone his highest vocation, also promotes his dignity and gives birth to community, based on the gospel proclamation being welcomed, interiorised, celebrated and lived.

Make us worthy, Lord,
to serve those throughout the world
who live and die in poverty and hunger.
Give them through our hands,
this day their daily bread,
and by our understanding love, give peace and joy.
Amen.

Pope Paul VI (1897-1978)

...as the Lord told him

Few of us appreciate being told what to do. Moreover, being obedient is often equated with weakness, submission, defeat or a lack of freedom. Yet Abraham's obedience was rooted in faith, a faith that knew everything about trust and hope, a faith that inspired others to follow him. It was by this faith that Abraham obeyed the call to become a pilgrim and a stranger in a new land. We are called to live our lives through this lens of faith, to trust in God's faithfulness and hope in God's goodness.

From Centesimus Annus (Centenary of Pope Leo XIII's encyclical on Capital and Labour)

51. Sacred Scripture continually speaks to us of an active commitment to our neighbour and demands of us a shared responsibility for all of humanity. This duty is not limited to one's own family, nation or State, but extends progressively to all mankind, since no one can consider himself extraneous or indifferent to the lot of another member of the human family. No one can say that he is not responsible for the well-being of his brother or sister (cf. Genesis 4:9; Luke 10:29-37; Matthew 25:31-46).

Make us worthy, Lord,
to serve those throughout the world
who live and die in poverty and hunger.
Give them through our hands,
this day their daily bread,
and by our understanding love, give peace and joy.
Amen.

Pope Paul VI (1897-1978)

Jesus came to the Samaritan town called Sychar, near the land that Jacob gave to his son Joseph. Jacob's well is there and Jesus, tired by the journey, sat straight down by the well. It was about the sixth hour. When a Samaritan woman came to draw water, Jesus said to her, 'Give me a drink.' His disciples had gone into the town to buy food. The Samaritan woman said to him, 'What? You are a Jew and you ask me, a Samaritan, for a drink?' – Jews, in fact, do not associate with Samaritans.

Jesus replied: 'If you only knew what God is offering and who it is that is saying to you: 'Give me a drink', you would have been the one to ask, and he would have given you living water.' 'You have no bucket, sir,' she answered, 'and the well is deep: how would you get this living water? Are you a greater man than our father Jacob who gave us this well and drank from it himself with his sons and his cattle?' Jesus replied: 'Whoever drinks this water will get thirsty again; but anyone who drinks the water that I shall give will never be thirsty again: the water that I shall give will turn into a spring inside him, welling up to eternal life.'

'Sir,' said the woman, 'give me some of that water, so that I may never get thirsty and never have to come here again to draw water. I see you are a prophet, sir' said the woman. 'Our fathers worshipped on this mountain, while you say that Jerusalem is the place where one ought to worship.'

Jesus said: 'Believe me, woman, the hour is coming when you will worship the Father neither on this mountain nor in Jerusalem. You worship what you do not know; we worship what we do know; for salvation comes from the Jews. But the hour will come – in fact it is here already – when true worshippers will worship the Father in spirit and truth: that is the kind of worshipper the Father wants. God is spirit, and those who worship must worship in spirit and truth.'

Then the woman said to him, 'I know that Messiah – that is, Christ – is coming; and when he comes he will tell us everything.' 'I who am speaking to you,' said Jesus, 'I am he.' Many Samaritans of that town had believed in him on the strength of the woman's testimony when she said, 'He told me all I have ever done,' so, when the Samaritans came up to him, they begged him to stay with them. He stayed for two days, and when he spoke to them many more came to believe; and they said to the woman, 'Now we no longer believe because of what you told us; we have heard him ourselves and we know that he really is the saviour of the world.'

John 4:5-15, 19-26, 39-42

Whom do we turn to in times of difficulty, when we thirst? How often do we turn to God? Are we available to others in their times of need?

Jesus, the foreigner, opened himself to the locals by starting a conversation, by braking the ice. How can we respond to his challenge and follow his example?

Make us worthy, Lord,
to serve those throughout the world
who live and die in poverty and hunger.
Give them through our hands,
this day their daily bread,
and by our understanding love, give peace and joy.
Amen.

Pope Paul VI (1897-1978)

Opening Prayer

Leader: When Israel went out from Egypt,
the house of Jacob from a people of strange language,
Judah became God's sanctuary,
Israel his dominion.

Group: **The sea looked and fled;**
Jordan turned back.
The mountains skipped like rams,
the hills like lambs.

Leader: Why is it, O sea, that you flee?
O Jordan, that you turn back?
O mountains, that you skip like rams?
O hills, like lambs?

Group: **Tremble, O earth, at the presence of the Lord,**
at the presence of the God of Jacob,
who turns the rock into a pool of water,
the flint into a spring of water.

From Psalm 114

All: **Glory be to the Father...**

Leader: Lord, in this moment of silence
help us to be still
so that your word may enter our minds,
touch our hearts,
and direct our lives to you.

After a short silence the group or an individual says:

Gracious and holy Father,
give us wisdom to perceive you,
intelligence to understand you,
diligence to seek you,
patience to wait for you,
eyes to behold you,
a heart to meditate on you,
and a life to proclaim you;
through the power of the
Spirit of Jesus Christ our Lord,
Amen.

St. Benedict of Nursia (c.480-c.547)

Explore the Sunday Scriptures - Third Sunday of Lent (Exodus 17: 3-7)

Tormented by thirst, the people complained against Moses. 'Why did you bring us out of Egypt?' they said. 'Was it so that I should die of thirst, my children too, and my cattle?' Moses appealed to the Lord. 'How am I to deal with this people?' he said. 'A little more and they will stone me!' The Lord said to Moses, 'Take with you some of the elders of Israel and move on to the forefront of the people, take in your hand the staff with which you struck the river, and go. I shall be standing before you there on the rock, at Horeb. You must strike the rock, and water will flow from it for the people to drink.' This is what Moses did, in the sight of the elders of Israel. The place was named Massah and Meribah because of the grumbling of the sons of Israel and because they put the Lord to the test by saying, 'Is the Lord with us, or not?'

Following a short period of silence you may wish to share an image, a thought, a phrase, a question that has struck you.

For Reflection

In this passage from Exodus the people of Israel can be found in the wilderness tormented by thirst, and fearful for their own lives and for the lives of their children and cattle. 'Is the Lord with us, or not?', they ask. Moses turns to the Lord, the Lord listens and the Lord quenches their thirst.

A similar theme is taken up in the gospel for the Third Sunday of Lent (John 4:5-15. 19-26, 39-42). At first it seems that it is Christ who thirsts and that the thirst in question is a physical one. Certainly, he approaches the Samaritan woman at the well and asks her for water. However, by the end of this encounter, Christ has still not received any water. On the contrary it is the Samaritan woman who receives something from Christ; not physical water from the well, but that spiritual nourishment that will lead to eternal life.

Clearly, physical needs cannot be ignored, but it is all too easy to interpret need in purely physical terms. As basic as food, shelter and clothing might be, other needs can be equally pressing; the need to be heard and to belong as well as the intellectual, cultural, social, emotional and spiritual needs that contribute to our sense of well being. For the Christian another's hunger cannot be ignored, but our concern is much more than a humanitarian one. We are called to proclaim Christ; in the desert of need it is he alone who is the answer to the deepest longings of the human heart.

On the part of individuals and communities, the welcome afforded the migrant, as to any newcomer, requires an attentive ear, a careful listening, an open heart. In recognising the complexity of human need we share in the ministry that Christ exercised at the well. Another person's needs cannot be presumed because need comes in all shapes and sizes. In fact, it may even be that the greatest act of welcome is not that practical assistance so easily given.

Share your thoughts on this reflection. How does this week's Scripture reading and reflection encourage you? Where are you affirmed? Where are you challenged? What impact might this have on your daily living?

From Erga migrantes caritas Christi

39. Migration therefore touches the religious dimension of man too and offers Catholic migrants a privileged though often painful opportunity to reach a sense of belonging to the universal Church which goes beyond any local particularity. To this end it is important that communities do not think that they have completed their duty to migrants simply by performing acts of fraternal assistance or even by supporting legislation aimed at giving them their due place in society while respecting their identity as foreigners. Christians must in fact promote an authentic culture of welcome capable of accepting the truly human values of the immigrants over and above any difficulties caused by living together with persons who are different.

Leader: Aloud or in the silence of our hearts let us bring to the Father our thanks (pause)…

Leader: In sorrow let us ask the Father for forgiveness (pause)…

Leader: With confidence let us entrust to the Father our cares and concerns (pause)…

Closing Prayer

Lord, forgive us the times we have ignored those in need,
or refused a welcome to those you have embraced.
Strengthen us with your grace, open our hearts,
that our thoughts, words and deeds,
may reflect your love for the neighbours you set before us,
for you live and reign with the Father and the Holy Spirit,
one God, for ever and ever.
Amen.

Who is My Neighbour?

My neighbour's needs are not to be presumed.

My neighbour is someone to be listened to.

My neighbour has an insight into what it is he or she needs.

My neighbour is not someone to be labelled and forgotten.

**Read the Scripture from the Third Sunday of Lent (Year A) -
Exodus 17: 3-7**

The version used at Mass can be found at the beginning of the Group
Session for Week Three (p.36). You may, of course, read from your own Bible.

Background

As with the book of Genesis, Exodus (the Greek term Exodus means
'going forth') was edited by the priestly school on their return to
Jerusalem from exile in Babylon in the sixth century BC. This return
was seen, theologically, as God's gracious act of salvation towards Israel
(prophesied by Isaiah in c. 560 BC; see, e.g. Isaiah 49: 6). On this basis,
therefore, the Jerusalem priests reflected on the earlier action of God in
releasing his people from slavery in Egypt in c. 1220s BC. In the Exodus
narrative the action of God is demonstrated by Israel's safe crossing of
the Red Sea (Exodus 15: 15-31), the giving of the divine Law (Heb. Torah,
Exodus 19: 16-25) and the offer of settlement in 'the land of promise'
(Exodus. 6: 4). Central to the unfolding of this narrative is the
personality of Moses who exercises his ministry in the strength of
Yahweh's divine commission (Exodus 3: 1-12).

As with the Israelite exile, the Exodus narrative is told in terms of the
dual theme of judgement and restoration. God is restoring his people
but frequently they disobey him. Given the redemption they received
through the Red Sea experience, on their journey through the
wilderness the people forsake the divine commandment and complain
about their treatment. The issue in Exodus 17 concerns the provision
of water. Despite Israel's murmuring, God remains gracious. Before the
holy mountain of Horeb they receive water. Israel, however, must be
reminded continuously of the precise geographical location of her
complaining. The place is named by the Hebrew terms Massah (trial)
and Meribah (contention). This tradition entered into the liturgical life
of Israel through the recitation of Psalm 95 (94 in the Vulgate) vv. 8-9

which explains why the forty years in the wilderness was a period of disobedience which angered God and why the original Exodus pilgrims did not enter 'the land of promise' (Psalm 95: 11).

O God, send forth your Holy Spirit
into my heart that I may perceive,
into my mind that I may remember,
and into my soul that I may meditate.
Inspire me to speak with piety, holiness,
tenderness and mercy.
Teach, guide and direct my thoughts and senses
from beginning to end.
May your grace ever help and correct me,
and may I be strengthened now with wisdom from on high,
for the sake of your infinite mercy.
Amen.

St. Anthony of Padua (c.1195-1231)

Tormented by thirst

Crossing the desert was a test of faith for those who travelled with Moses. They were tormented by the lack of water for their children, their animals and themselves. We too can thirst, but for what? We can thirst for acceptance and belonging – the desire to feel at home – and faced with discrimination and division we can thirst for justice and equality. As the Israelites thirsted for water in the desert and their thirst was quenched, how often do we thirst for that strength and courage to imitate Christ's example?

From the Compendium of the Catechism

592. What is the sense of the petition 'Give us this day our daily bread'? Asking God with the filial trust of children for the daily nourishment which is necessary for us all we recognise how good God is, beyond all goodness. We ask also for the grace to know how to act so that justice and solidarity may allow the abundance of some to remedy the needs of others.

O God, send forth your Holy Spirit
into my heart that I may perceive,
into my mind that I may remember,
and into my soul that I may meditate.
Inspire me to speak with piety, holiness,
tenderness and mercy.
Teach, guide and direct my thoughts and senses
from beginning to end.
May your grace ever help and correct me,
and may I be strengthened now with wisdom from on high,
for the sake of your infinite mercy.
Amen.

St. Anthony of Padua (c.1195-1231)

There are still many Catholics like me who feel that going to a Catholic Church is like joining a family, having your own community in a strange country, some place where you belong.

Italian woman from The Ground of Justice

From Gaudium et Spes

24. God, Who has fatherly concern for everyone, has willed that all men should constitute one family and treat one another in a spirit of brotherhood. For having been created in the image of God, Who 'from one man has created the whole human race and made them live all over the face of the earth' (Acts 17:26), all men are called to one and the same goal, namely God Himself.

O God, send forth your Holy Spirit
into my heart that I may perceive,
into my mind that I may remember,
and into my soul that I may meditate.
Inspire me to speak with piety, holiness,
tenderness and mercy.
Teach, guide and direct my thoughts and senses
from beginning to end.
May your grace ever help and correct me,
and may I be strengthened now with wisdom from on high,
for the sake of your infinite mercy.
Amen.

St. Anthony of Padua (c. 1195-1231)

I shall be standing there before you

In 1943, psychologist Abraham Maslow outlined a 'hierarchy of needs', ranging from the basic physical needs of food and drink to security. For Maslow it is only once these basic needs are met that the person is able to pursue the 'ultimate goal' of self-realisation. We all have particular needs that need satisfying, whether they are the need for basic security and housing or a need for recognition or love. If creating a list of things we need to be happy, what would come at the top? Would we start our lists with the basics, food and water, or suggest something else? Would the key to our happiness be friendships and a satisfaction borne of a well-developed relationship with God? God's promise to Moses was that he would be there at Horeb. In more than one way we find God before us, there to satisfy our needs. He is there in the person of those around us, both familiar and new; in the community gathered at church and in the Spirit Christ promised to his Church.

From Erga migrantes caritas Christi

6. The precarious situation of so many foreigners, which should arouse everyone's solidarity, instead brings about fear in many, who feel that immigrants are a burden, regard them with suspicion and even consider them a danger and a threat. This often provokes manifestations of intolerance, xenophobia and racism.

O God, send forth your Holy Spirit
into my heart that I may perceive,
into my mind that I may remember,
and into my soul that I may meditate.
Inspire me to speak with piety, holiness,
tenderness and mercy.
Teach, guide and direct my thoughts and senses
from beginning to end.
May your grace ever help and correct me,
and may I be strengthened now with wisdom from on high,
for the sake of your infinite mercy.
Amen.

St. Anthony of Padua (c.1195-1231)

I work in a shop. I am paid £3.50 per hour. On average I work 60 hours a week. From this I pay the shop owner for accommodation in one of the houses he owns. With food included this costs me £60 per week. I send some money home to my family as I have a sister and a mother. It costs me quite a lot if I go to Western Union. I try to send the money with friends. Sometimes it does not all get there. I came here for the family. I do not speak English. I like my church. It gives me spiritual help. It makes me feel safe. I cannot always go on Sunday because I always work. I have a shrine in my room. I pray every day.

Sri Lankan migrant – this man was unaware of the minimum wage and unsure if he had the right papers to be in the country now.
Taken from *The Ground of Justice*

From Erga migrantes caritas Christi

39 ...it is important that communities do not think that they have completed their duty to migrants simply by performing acts of fraternal assistance or even by supporting legislation aimed at giving them their due place in society while respecting their identity as foreigners. Christians must in fact promote an authentic culture of welcome capable of accepting the truly human values of the immigrants over and above any difficulties caused by living together with persons who are different.

O God, send forth your Holy Spirit
into my heart that I may perceive,
into my mind that I may remember,
and into my soul that I may meditate.
Inspire me to speak with piety, holiness,
tenderness and mercy.
Teach, guide and direct my thoughts and senses
from beginning to end.
May your grace ever help and correct me,
and may I be strengthened now with wisdom from on high,
for the sake of your infinite mercy.
Amen.

St. Anthony of Padua (c.1195-1231)

'Is the Lord with us, or not?'

The grumbling of the sons of Israel was halted by the gift of water, their 'wanting' came, in part, from a feeling of abandonment and isolation. What they had taken for granted, though a life of servitude, was abandoned to trust. So often this experience is mirrored in the stories of those arriving from foreign shores, isolation is a very real cross to bear. There are the 'higher' needs than the purely physical – the need for recognition, friendship and love. The stresses and strains we are faced with will be diminished when we recognise of God's love and the support he offers us through others. What is true now was true in the twelfth century when St. Aelred of Rivaulx wrote: 'medicine is not more powerful or more efficacious for our wounds in all our temporal needs than the possession of a friend who meets misfortune joyfully, so that, as the Apostle says, shoulder to shoulder, they bear one another's burdens… the best medicine in life is a friend.'

From Erga migrantes caritas Christi

16. In the early Church, hospitality was the Christians' response to the needs of itinerant missionaries, of religious leaders in exile or on a journey, and of poor members of various communities.

O God, send forth your Holy Spirit
into my heart that I may perceive,
into my mind that I may remember,
and into my soul that I may meditate.
Inspire me to speak with piety, holiness,
tenderness and mercy.
Teach, guide and direct my thoughts and senses
from beginning to end.
May your grace ever help and correct me,
and may I be strengthened now with wisdom from on high,
for the sake of your infinite mercy.
Amen.

St. Anthony of Padua (c. 1195-1231)

As Jesus went along, he saw a man who had been blind from birth. He spat on the ground, made a paste with the spittle, put this over the eyes of the blind man and said to him, 'Go and wash in the Pool of Siloam' (a name that means 'sent'). So the blind man went off and washed himself, and came away with his sight restored.

His neighbours and people who earlier had seen him begging said, 'Isn't this the man who used to sit and beg?' Some said, 'Yes, it is the same one.' Others said, 'No, he only looks like him.' The man himself said, 'I am the man.'

They brought the man who had been blind to the Pharisees. It had been a sabbath day when Jesus made the paste and opened the man's eyes, so when the Pharisees asked him how he had come to see, he said, "He put a paste on my eyes, and I washed, and I can see." Then some of the Pharisees said, 'This man cannot be from God: he does not keep the sabbath.' Others said, 'How could a sinner produce signs like this?' And there was disagreement among them. So they spoke to the blind man again, 'What have you to say about him yourself, now that he has opened your eyes?' 'He is a prophet,' replied the man. 'Are you trying to teach us,' they replied, 'and you a sinner through and through, since you were born!' And they drove him away.

Jesus heard they had driven him away, and when he found him he said to him, 'Do you believe in the Son of Man?' 'Sir,' the man replied, 'tell me who he is so that I may believe in him.' Jesus said, 'You are looking at him; he is speaking to you.' The man said, 'Lord, I believe,' and worshipped him.

John 9:1, 6-9, 13-17, 34-38

In the face of all his difficulties the man born blind confessed to his belief in Jesus, the Christ. During times of hardship and times of plenty do you believe in the Son of Man?

O God, send forth your Holy Spirit
into my heart that I may perceive,
into my mind that I may remember,
and into my soul that I may meditate.
Inspire me to speak with piety, holiness,
tenderness and mercy.
Teach, guide and direct my thoughts and senses
from beginning to end.
May your grace ever help and correct me,
and may I be strengthened now with wisdom from on high,
for the sake of your infinite mercy.
Amen.

St. Anthony of Padua (c. 1195-1231)

Opening Prayer

Leader:	Praise the Lord, all you nations! Extol him, all you peoples!
Group:	**For great is his steadfast love toward us, and the faithfulness of the Lord endures forever.**
Leader:	Praise the Lord!

From Psalm 117

All:	**Glory be to the Father…**
Leader:	Lord, in this moment of silence help us to be still so that your word may enter our minds, touch our hearts, and direct our lives to you.

After a short silence the group or an individual says:

Gracious and holy Father,
give us wisdom to perceive you,
intelligence to understand you,
diligence to seek you,
patience to wait for you,
eyes to behold you,
a heart to meditate on you,
and a life to proclaim you;
through the power of the
Spirit of Jesus Christ our Lord,
Amen.

St. Benedict of Nursia (c.480-c.547)

Explore the Sunday Scriptures from the Fourth Sunday of Lent (1 Samuel 16: 1, 6-7,10-13)

The Lord said to Samuel, 'Fill your horn with oil and go. I am sending you to Jesse of Bethlehem, for I have chosen myself a king among his sons.' When Samuel arrived, he caught sight of Eliab and thought, 'Surely the Lord's anointed one stands there before him,' but the Lord said to Samuel, 'Take no notice of his appearance or his height for I have rejected him; God does not see as man sees; man looks at appearances but the Lord looks at the heart.' Jesse presented his seven sons to Samuel, but Samuel said to Jesse, 'The Lord has not chosen these.' He then asked Jesse, 'Are these all the sons you have?' he answered, 'There is still one left, the youngest; he is out looking after the sheep.' Then Samuel said to Jesse, 'Send for him; we will not sit down to eat until he comes.' Jesse had him sent for, a boy of fresh complexion, with fine eyes and pleasant bearing. The Lord said, 'Come, anoint him, for this is the one.' At this, Samuel took the horn of oil and anointed him where he stood with his brothers; and the spirit of the Lord seized on David and stayed with him from that day on.

Following a short period of silence you may wish to share an image, a thought, a phrase, a question that has struck you.

For Reflection

Just as Samuel was initially struck by appearances, society today puts great emphasis on appearances. In any given industry businesses try to create the impression of our needing a particular product to look, to be or to feel good. However, beauty – real beauty – has little to do with cosmetics, or fashion. The beauty of each individual lies in our being made in the likeness of our Creator.

The challenge for each of us, whether we are the person welcoming or the one who has newly arrived, is to see beyond appearances. In the passage we have just listened to David is described as 'a boy of fresh complexion, with fine eyes and pleasant bearing' but he was not chosen for his good looks; he was chosen because the Lord had looked into his heart. Knowing David, the Lord discerned for him a particular path or vocation. Seeing beyond appearances, we can begin to see as God sees; recognising, as Samuel, Jesse, Eliab and his brothers did, what it is that another has to offer and which God, in his graciousness, sets before us. Just as each person has a unique combination of genes that translate into their own individual attributes, God has gifted each of us with particular talents and abilities. Our faith not only asks us to imitate Christ to the best of these abilities but also to offer our talents for the good of all our brothers and sisters in Christ.

We are not all called to be kings or rulers, but as Cardinal John Henry Newman reminds us, we all have some definite service to perform. In the migrant, the Church is presented with a unique opportunity to remember its beginnings at Pentecost (when peoples from different nations were addressed in their own language) and its vocation (to build up the Body of Christ). In the migrant we are offered a wonderful opportunity to explore afresh that fulfilment of communion and mission which lies at the heart of what it is for the Church to be Church. Yes, we can welcome the 'stranger' or the 'migrant', anxious to tell him or her how things are done, to get him or her to do what 'we' do, but in doing so we can be oblivious to what he or she has to teach us?

Share your thoughts on this reflection. How does this week's Scripture reading and reflection encourage you? Where are you affirmed? Where are you challenged? What impact might this have on your daily living?

From Erga migrantes caritas Christi

103. Migrants, too, can be the hidden providential builders of…a universal fraternity together with many other brothers and sisters. They offer the Church the opportunity to realise more concretely its identity as communion and its missionary vocation, as asserted by the Vicar of Christ

(Pope John Paul II): "Migrations offer individual local Churches the opportunity to verify their catholicity, which consists not only in welcoming different ethnic groups, but above all in creating communion with them and among them. Ethnic and cultural pluralism in the Church is not just something to be tolerated because it is transitory, it is a structural dimension. The unity of the Church is not given by a common origin and language but by the Spirit of Pentecost which, bringing together men and women of different languages and nations in one people, confers on them all faith in the same Lord and the calling to the same hope."

Leader:	Aloud or in the silence of our hearts let us bring to the Father our thanks (pause)…
Leader:	In sorrow let us ask the Father for forgiveness (pause)…
Leader:	With confidence let us entrust to the Father our cares and concerns (pause)…

Closing Prayer

Lord, forgive us the times we have ignored those in need,
or refused a welcome to those you have embraced.
Strengthen us with your grace, open our hearts,
that our thoughts, words and deeds,
may reflect your love for the neighbours you set before us,
for you live and reign with the Father and the Holy Spirit,
one God, for ever and ever.
Amen.

Who is My Neighbour?

My neighbour is unique in the sight of God.
My neighbour has something definite to offer.
My neighbour is God's gift to me in this place, at this time.
My neighbour is the challenge to see as God sees.

Read the Scripture from the Fourth Sunday of Lent (Year A) - I Samuel 16: 1, 6-7, 10-13

The version used at Mass can be found at the beginning of the Group Session for Week Four (p.53). You may, of course, read from your own Bible.

Background

Prior to the establishment of the 'priestly school' in the sixth century BC there existed another group of theologians who can be categorised as the 'Deuteronomic School'. This group reinterpreted Israel's historical and theological traditions in terms of the principles found in Moses' final sermon to Israel in the book of Deuteronomy (the Greek term Deuteronomy means second law). Part of the Deuteronomists' concern was with the political life of Israel. In the sixth century they questioned whether or not the monarchy (a type of government found from c. 1020 - 586 BC) should be restored (cf. Deuteronomy 17: 14 - 20). Despite their investigation of the origins of the Davidic monarchy (they believed that David, c. 1000 - 960 BC represented the ideal king) the monarchy was not restored in the post-exilic age but the 'Davidic spirit' remained (see, Haggai 1: 1). In I Samuel 16 David's election as king was prophetically inspired through the ministry of Samuel following his rejection of the leadership of Saul (I Samuel 15: 10 - 11). Samuel is instructed by Yahweh to journey to the family of Jesse in Bethlehem (I Samuel 16: 1) where Samuel is to appoint a king from amongst Jesse's sons. In this context David's election, as a result of his humility and apparent inferiority (I Samuel 16: 11), is ironical in that it was he who obtained the divine favour by being endowed with Yahweh's spirit for kingly rule (I Samuel 16: 13). This anointing marks the beginning of David's rise to kingship. His occupation as a shepherd (I Samuel 16: 11) reveals his future pastoral role in the protection of his people, Psalm 72 (71 in the Vulgate) vv. 12 - 13, while the subsequent reflection on his monarchy in relation to God is represented liturgically by other 'Royal psalms' (see, for example, Psalm 2: 7).

O Lord our God,
help us to realise our dependence on one another
each dispensing and receiving the graces and gifts you bestow remembering that,
unless we do this for love of You, it is worth nothing.
Amen

Adapted from the Dialogue of Saint Catherine of Siena (1347-1380)

I have chosen myself a king

Out of all of the sons of Jesse, strong and honourable though they undoubtedly were, the Lord chose David. David, the youngest, a shepherd boy, was chosen to be king of God's chosen people. So out of the least of the tribes of Israel come not one but two kings, David the mighty warrior king, good and just, and Jesus, the Christ, the Messiah. From the very least can come the very best. Recognising the gifts of others can be difficult but is of great importance. All have gifts given by the Giver who looks not at appearances, but at the heart (1 Samuel 1:7).

From Novo Millennio Ineunte

43. A spirituality of communion implies also the ability to see what is positive in others, to welcome it and prize it as a gift from God: not only as a gift for the brother or sister who has received it directly, but also as a 'gift for me'.

O Lord our God,
help us to realise our dependence on one another
each dispensing and receiving the graces and gifts you bestow
remembering that, unless we do this for love of You, it is worth nothing.
Amen

Adapted from the Dialogue of Saint Catherine of Siena (1347-1380)

There are always ups and downs in this country. You try to find a job, you try to go to school... But no matter what education you have, no matter how able you are, there is always that boundary, that line of segregation when you are told: you know what, I know you can do this, I know you are good, but... For example, you put in your CV for a job application. If you are invited for an interview, from the moment you walk in the door you are dependent on luck... 'Where are you from? Nigeria? Ok, we will call you, don't bother calling us back'. This is an everyday experience. You walk on the street and people look at you thinking that everybody who is black has got a gun... At work, your boss who probably has a primary or secondary education, looks down at you even if you've got a degree... They tell you – yes, you can be in this country, but... you are not given the chance for improvement - they don't want you to grow.

From interviews undertaken for The Ground of Justice

From Novo Millennio Ineunte

86. In both the Church and society the lay faithful, lay associations and ecclesial movements, with all the diversity of their charisms and ministries, are called to bear Christian witness and to be in the service of migrants too. In particular we have in mind pastoral assistants and catechists, animators of groups of young people or adults, persons engaged in the world of labour, in social and charitable services. In a Church that strives to be entirely missionary-ministerial, urged by the Spirit, respect for the gifts of all must be given prominence. In this matter the lay faithful enjoy areas of rightful autonomy, but they also take on typical tasks of *diakonia* (service), such as visiting the sick, helping the elderly, leading youth groups, animating family associations, teaching catechism and holding courses of professional qualification, working in schools and in administration and, furthermore, helping in the liturgy and in 'consultation centres', in prayer meetings and in meditation on the Word of God.

O Lord our God,
help us to realise our dependence on one another
each dispensing and receiving the graces and gifts you bestow
remembering that, unless we do this for love of You, it is worth nothing.
Amen

Adapted from the Dialogue of Saint Catherine of Siena (1347-1380)

God does not see as man sees

St. Benedict wrote the following in his Rule – 'All who arrive as guests are to be welcomed like Christ, for he is going to say, "I was a stranger and you welcomed me (Matthew 25:35)." A guest should be met with every expression of charity'. The 'stranger' presents us with a chance for renewal. In the 'stranger' we can meet Christ, while in our attitude and actions towards others we have an opportunity to imitate Christ. Let Christ in them be an example to us on our shared journey.

From Novo Millennio Ineunte

43. A spirituality of communion indicates above all the heart's contemplation of the mystery of the Trinity dwelling in us, and whose light we must also be able to see shining on the face of the brothers and sisters around us. A spirituality of communion also means an ability to think of our brothers and sisters in faith within the profound unity of the Mystical Body, and therefore as 'those who are a part of me'. This makes us able to share their joys and sufferings, to sense their desires and attend to their needs, to offer them deep and genuine friendship.

O Lord our God,
help us to realise our dependence on one another
each dispensing and receiving the graces and gifts you bestow
remembering that, unless we do this for love of You, it is worth nothing.
Amen

Adapted from the Dialogue of Saint Catherine of Siena (1347-1380)

My deafness is a stumbling block which causes communication problems when I attend Masses in churches, as opposed to Deaf Masses. It is hard to follow the priest when he gives his homily and I have always felt uncomfortable being unable to follow what was being said in the Mass, only following other people's movements. I would appreciate a printed sheet outlining important parts or news announcements. Generally, I have no problems with society, and I can feel welcome once I reveal my deafness. As for the Church, I can feel welcomed but not included on account of my deafness thus a lack of conversation. Because of this lack of communication I lack the opportunity to share my talents with the parish and those around me.

Ian Urquhart, member of the Westminster Deaf Community

From the Committee for the Jubilee Day of the Community with Persons with Disabilities (December 2000)

The richness of a person with disability is a constant challenge to the Church and society to open to the mystery such persons present. The person with disabilities has rights and duties like every other individual. Disability is not a punishment, it is a place where normality and stereotypes are challenged and the Church and society are moved to search for that crucial point at which the human person is fully himself. It is in this spirit that we entrust this preparation to all of you, in view of the full integration and inclusion of persons with disabilities in the life of the Church and society, to give value to the gifts they bring, to reconcile ourselves with them for failings in their regard in the spirit of the Great Jubilee and to encourage an attitude of caring, assistance and solidarity.

O Lord our God,
help us to realise our dependence on one another
each dispensing and receiving the graces and gifts you bestow
remembering that, unless we do this for love of You, it is worth nothing.
Amen

Adapted from the Dialogue of Saint Catherine of Siena (1347-1380)

Come, anoint him

In the Catholic Christian tradition oils are used during the administration of the Sacraments. In baptism, confirmation and ordination it is used to highlight the dignity of the vocation to which the anointed has been called. In David's case it was a call to kingship, a life of service to God's chosen people. As a king, David's task was to hold the community together. The 'royal priesthood' we are called to in baptism confers a kingship on each and every one of us. We too are called to be builders of *communio*, a community where there is no 'distinction between Greek and Jew, slave and free man' (Colossians 3:11), a community characterised by a love that is 'always patient and kind, never jealous, boastful or conceited'…a love which 'delights in the truth, always ready to excuse, to trust, to hope and to endure whatever comes' (1 Corinthians 13:4, 6).

From Novo Millennio Ineunte

43. A spirituality of communion means, finally, to know how to 'make room' for our brothers and sisters, bearing 'each other's burdens' (Galatians 6:2) and resisting the selfish temptations which constantly beset us and provoke competition, careerism, distrust and jealousy. Let us have no illusions: unless we follow this spiritual path, external structures of communion will serve very little purpose. They would become mechanisms without a soul, 'masks' of communion rather than its means of expression and growth.

O Lord our God,
help us to realise our dependence on one another
each dispensing and receiving the graces and gifts you bestow
remembering that, unless we do this for love of You, it is worth nothing.
Amen

Adapted from the Dialogue of Saint Catherine of Siena (1347-1380)

The sisters Martha and Mary sent this message to Jesus, 'Lord, the man you love is ill.' On receiving the message, Jesus said, 'This sickness will not end in death but in God's glory, and through it the Son of God will be glorified.'

Jesus loved Martha and her sister and Lazarus, yet when he learned that Lazarus was ill he stayed where he was for two more days before saying to the disciples, 'Let us go to Judea.'

On arriving, Jesus found that Lazarus had been in the tomb for four days already. When Martha heard that Jesus had come she went to meet him. Mary remained sitting in the house. Martha said to Jesus, 'If you had been here, my brother would not have died, but I know that even now, whatever you ask of God, he will grant you.' 'Your brother' said Jesus to her 'will rise again.' Martha said, 'I know he will rise again at the resurrection on the last day.' Jesus said:

'I am the resurrection and the life.
If anyone believes in me, even though he dies he will live,
and whoever lives and believes in me
will never die.
Do you believe this?'

'Yes Lord,' she said 'I believe that you are the Christ, the Son of God, the one who was to come into this world.' Jesus said in great distress, with a sigh that came straight from the heart, 'Where have you put him?' They said, 'See how much he loved him!' But there were some who remarked, 'He opened the eyes of the blind man, could he not have prevented this man's death?' Still sighing, Jesus reached the tomb; it was a cave with a stone to close the opening. Jesus said, 'Take the stone away.' Martha said to him, 'Lord, by now he will smell; this is the fourth day.' Jesus replied, 'Have I not told you that if you believe you will see the glory of God?' So they took away the stone. Then Jesus lifted up his eyes and said:

'Father, I thank you for hearing my prayer.
I knew indeed that you always hear me,
but I speak for the sake of all these who stand round me,
so that they may believe it was you who sent me.'

When he had said this, he cried in a loud voice, 'Lazarus, here! Come out!
The dead man came out, his feet and hands bound with bands of stuff and
a cloth round his face. Jesus said to them, 'Unbind him, let him go free.'

Many of the Jews who had come to visit Mary and had seen what he did
believed in him.

John 11:3-7, 17, 20-27, 33-45

*Do we trust that the Lord will answer our prayers as he did that day with
Martha and Mary? Are there any attitudes that keep us bound? Do we need to
be freed from any prejudices?*

O Lord our God,
help us to realise our dependence on one another
each dispensing and receiving the graces and gifts you bestow
remembering that, unless we do this for love of You, it is worth nothing.
Amen

Adapted from the Dialogue of Saint Catherine of Siena (1347-1380)

Opening Prayer

Leader:

When they were few in number,
of little account, and strangers in it,
wandering from nation to nation,
from one kingdom to another people,

Group:

**he allowed no one to oppress them;
he rebuked kings on their account,
saying, 'Do not touch my anointed ones;
do my prophets no harm.'…
He had sent a man ahead of them,
Joseph, who was sold as a slave…**

Leader:

He sent his servant Moses,
and Aaron whom he had chosen.
They performed his signs among them,
and miracles in the land of Ham…

Group:

**Then he brought Israel out with silver and gold,
and there was no one among their tribes
who stumbled…
He spread a cloud for a covering,
and fire to give light by night.**

Leader:

They asked, and he brought quails,
and gave them food from heaven in abundance.
He opened the rock, and water gushed out…
So he brought his people out with joy,
his chosen ones with singing…

From Psalm 105

All:

Glory be to the Father…

Leader: Lord, in this moment of silence
            help us to be still
            so that your word may enter our minds,
            touch our hearts,
            and direct our lives to you.

After a short silence the group or an individual says:

Gracious and holy Father,
give us wisdom to perceive you,
intelligence to understand you,
diligence to seek you,
patience to wait for you,
eyes to behold you,
a heart to meditate on you,
and a life to proclaim you;
through the power of the
Spirit of Jesus Christ our Lord,
Amen.

St. Benedict of Nursia (c.480-c.547)

Explore the Sunday Scriptures – Fifth Sunday of Lent (John 11:3-7, 17, 20-27, 33-45)

The sisters Martha and Mary sent this message to Jesus, 'Lord, the man you love is ill.' On receiving the message, Jesus said, 'This sickness will not end in death but in God's glory, and through it the Son of God will be glorified.'

Jesus loved Martha and her sister and Lazarus, yet when he learned that Lazarus was ill he stayed where he was for two more days before saying to the disciples, 'Let us go to Judea.'

On arriving, Jesus found that Lazarus had been in the tomb for four days already. When Martha heard that Jesus had come she went to meet him. Mary remained sitting in the house. Martha said to Jesus, 'If you had been here, my brother would not have died, but I know that even now, whatever you ask of God, he will grant you.' 'Your brother' said Jesus to her 'will rise again.' Martha said, 'I know he will rise again at the resurrection on the last day.' Jesus said:

'I am the resurrection and the life.
If anyone believes in me, even though he dies he will live,
and whoever lives and believes in me
will never die.
Do you believe this?'

'Yes Lord,' she said 'I believe that you are the Christ, the Son of God, the one who was to come into this world.' Jesus said in great distress, with a sigh that came straight from the heart, 'Where have you put him?' They said, 'See how much he loved him!' But there were some who remarked, 'He opened the eyes of the blind man, could he not have prevented this man's death?' Still sighing, Jesus reached the tomb; it was a cave with a stone to close the opening. Jesus said, 'Take the stone away.' Martha said to him, 'Lord, by now he will smell; this is the fourth day.' Jesus replied, 'Have I not told you that if you believe you will see the glory of God?' So they took away the stone. Then Jesus lifted up his eyes and said:

'Father, I thank you for hearing my prayer.
I knew indeed that you always hear me,
but I speak for the sake of all these who stand round me,
so that they may believe it was you who sent me.'

When he had said this, he cried in a loud voice, 'Lazarus, here! Come out! The dead man came out, his feet and hands bound with bands of stuff and a cloth round his face. Jesus said to them, 'Unbind him, let him go free.'

Many of the Jews who had come to visit Mary and had seen what he did believed in him.

Following a short period of silence you may wish to share an image, a thought, a phrase, a question that has struck you.

For Reflection

It is clear from the passage that Martha placed a great deal of trust in Jesus. 'If you had been here,' she says 'my brother would not have died'. It is also clear that she had good reason to trust him. He had already opened the eyes of the blind man. Ultimately, Christ's promise that Lazarus' sickness would not end in death 'but in God's glory' is realised. Always and everywhere there is a consistency in Christ's life. They knew he loved Lazarus because of the sigh that came straight from his heart and the tears he shed. His words, promises and actions were of a single piece. It is this link between word and action which proves convincing. It is this consistency, the bedrock of authenticity, which gives Christ credibility. Indeed, we are told at the end of the passage that many came to believe because they had seen what he did.

The welcome that we are called to offer to others is so much more than the non-committal handshake or cursory listening that first encounters can entail. It is more than a hymnbook, a smile and a copy of the newsletter. Certainly, these are necessary, but will only be meaningful where the welcome they speak of is a sincere one. How will the newcomer, migrant or otherwise, feel truly at home if all he or she has ever known is a wealth of good intentions; where they have been invited to contribute, but never been listened to, where their insight and energy have gone untapped, and parish priorities are reflective of the community as it used to be? The welcoming community is a community that actively makes room for others in all areas and at all levels of parish life. That said, everyone, both newcomers and the existing community are challenged by the same gospel, the same Christ to create this community of love and welcome.

Share your thoughts on this reflection. How does this week's Scripture reading and reflection encourage you? Where are you affirmed? Where are you challenged? What impact might this have on your daily living?

From Erga migrantes caritas Christi

43. Nevertheless assistance or 'first welcome' are of the greatest importance (let us think, for example, of migrants' hospitality centres, especially in transit countries) in response to the emergencies that come with migrations: canteens, dormitories, clinics, economic aid, reception centres. But also important are acts of welcome in its full sense, which aim at the progressive integration and self-sufficiency of the immigrant. Let us remember in particular the commitment undertaken for family unification, education of children, housing, work, associations, promotion of civil rights and migrants' various ways of participation in their host society. Religious, social, charitable and cultural associations of Christian inspiration should also make efforts to involve immigrants themselves in their structures.

Leader:	Aloud or in the silence of our hearts let us bring to the Father our thanks (pause)…
Leader:	In sorrow let us ask the Father for forgiveness (pause)…
Leader:	With confidence let us entrust to the Father our cares and concerns (pause)…

Closing prayer

Lord, forgive us the times we have ignored those in need,
or refused a welcome to those you have embraced.
Strengthen us with your grace, open our hearts,
that our thoughts, words and deeds,
may reflect your love for the neighbours you set before us,
for you live and reign with the Father and the Holy Spirit,
one God, for ever and ever.
Amen.

Who is My Neighbour?

My neighbour is a newcomer who challenges me to do things differently.
My neighbour is a newcomer to be welcomed with real deeds.
My neighbour is a newcomer with a voice to contribute.
My neighbour is a newcomer who belongs as much as I do.

Read the Scripture from the Fifth Sunday of Lent (Year A) - John 11:3-7, 17, 20-27, 33-45

The version used at Mass can be found at the beginning of the Group Session for Week Five (p. 68-70). You may, of course, read from your own Bible.

Background

Towards the end of the first century AD the author of the Fourth Gospel assembled historical and theological traditions about Jesus to meet the needs of his contemporary Christian congregation in their pastoral and evangelistic ministry (John 20:30-31).

He utilised previous gospel tradition and also was creative and innovative in his interpretation of that tradition seen in his stylistic arrangement: long discourses and dialogues designed to reveal theological profundity. John 11 forms the climax of the miraculous signs of Jesus which manifest his divine glory (John 2:11). One key to the interpretation of John 11 is to recognise the tensions in the passage seen, for example: first in the proclamation of Jesus' divinity (11:25) compared with his human response to the death of Lazarus (11:35). Secondly, the raising of Lazarus is a foretaste of the final resurrection of the faithful made possible by Jesus' own death (19:30-37) and resurrection (20:11-31). Thirdly, Jesus' act of love produces both belief and unbelief: as a result of the miraculous sign many Jews come to believe in Jesus (11:45) while the Jewish leaders plot to destroy him (11:53).

John's message, through the examination of these tensions, is clear: seeing Lazarus we see ourselves as partakers of the resurrection to eternal life which we can glimpse in the present time and, as a result, are lead to a deepening and stronger belief in Jesus as the unique Son of the Father (1:18) who inaugurates our salvation (20:30-31).

From Familiaris Consortio (The Family in the Modern World)

77. The families of migrants... should be able to find a homeland everywhere in the Church. This is a task stemming from the nature of the Church, as being the sign of unity in diversity. As far as possible these people should be looked after by priests of their own rite, culture and language. It is also the Church's task to appeal to the public conscience and to all those in authority in social, economic and political life, in order that workers may find employment in their own regions and homelands, that they may receive just wages, that their families may be reunited as soon as possible, be respected in their cultural identity and treated on an equal footing with others, and that their children may be given the chance to learn a trade and exercise it, as also the chance to own the land needed for working and living.

Lord Jesus Christ,
you told us that the one who asks will receive,
the one who seeks will find,
the one who knocks will have the door opened.
Grant us an understanding of your commands
and the strength to act upon them,
help us to treat others as we would like them to treat us,
for that is the meaning of the Law and the Prophets.
Amen.

Adapted from Matthew 7:7,12

When Martha heard that Jesus had come she went to meet him.

Even though Martha was distraught at the loss of her brother, she was able to move beyond and go out to greet the Lord. How hard it is to show welcome when we too are burdened. St. Paul in his letter to the Romans writes of an open and cordial hospitality 'If anyone of the Saints is in need, you must share with them, you must make hospitality your special care' (Romans 12:13). How often do we have 'good' excuses for not exercising that generosity that we are called to exercise? How do my own troubles blind me from my duty to others?

From Pope John Paul II's message on World Migration Day 1998

2. For the Christian, acceptance of and solidarity with the stranger are not only human duties of hospitality, but a precise demand of fidelity itself to Christ's teaching.

Lord Jesus Christ,
you told us that the one who asks will receive,
the one who seeks will find,
the one who knocks will have the door opened.
Grant us an understanding of your commands
and the strength to act upon them,
help us to treat others as we would like them to treat us,
for that is the meaning of the Law and the Prophets.
Amen.

Adapted from Matthew 7:7,12

I have progressed from mild to severe hearing impairment over 15 years. I still make use of hearing aids, loop systems, radio aids and lip-reading (constantly). One to one, quiet situations are best for me. Noisy gatherings, children's voices and distant speakers are challenging. My own faith experience, in spite of the increasing loss of hearing, does not deny God's acceptance of me. Jesus was wounded and we all have wounds.

In the deaf world we have a phrase: 'the nodding head syndrome'. This is usually accompanied by a smile and often indicates that the deafened person cannot hear a thing! To my deafened friends I would say don't pretend you have heard or understood. There are loads of good, caring people out there. Be honest and simple about your needs, let others know how to help. Learn assertiveness techniques; lip/face reading; equip your homes with suitable appliances; learn sign language (BSL), keep up with world news and don't avoid difficult situations.

To the parish I would say that there is a complicated range of deaf experiences, so take the time to listen to individual needs. Be caring about families with deafened children - 90% of deaf babies are born to hearing parents who have no experience of deafness. Take note of the elderly deaf - fiddly hearing aids can demoralise and end up for ever in the top drawer. Train your readers well, encourage the younger generation to learn sign language. Remember, deaf people love music, hymns and concerts, because the tones vary more than speech sounds, and are visually orientated. Print service sheets, perhaps homilies, wherever possible.

To my hearing neighbour I would say be ready to tell me what has been said later. Try not to say: 'it does not matter'. It does for me, I promise. Be patient. Speak clearly, not too fast and look at me. Rephrase the comment if I do not understand twice. Keep long hair away from your face, it prevents me face/lip reading. Use fax, email, letters, or visual means such as a textphone. Share a sense of humour with me. And finally…rejoice in the Lord always.

Sr Muriel Rowle

Lord Jesus Christ,
you told us that the one who asks will receive,
the one who seeks will find,
the one who knocks will have the door opened.
Grant us an understanding of your commands
and the strength to act upon them,
help us to treat others as we would like them to treat us,
for that is the meaning of the Law and the Prophets.
Amen.

Adapted from Matthew 7:7,12

Still sighing

Our words will not raise people from the dead and we may not be able to solve every difficulty that our neighbours face. Yet as Christ's sighing was a real expression of his love, the little that we can do can make an enormous difference. Think what time can be put aside to help check documents, explain letters or make a phone call on their behalf. More often than not our witness to Christ is not in the great or in the miraculous but in the ordinary. As Blessed Mother Theresa reminds us, 'we are not called to do great things only small things with great love.' 'Being there' speaks volumes and a hand on the shoulder can speak with an eloquence our words sometimes lack.

From Erga migrantes caritas Christi

18. Migrants' journeying can become a living sign of an eternal vocation, a constant stimulus to that hope which points to a future beyond this present world... an appeal for us to live again the fraternity of Pentecost, when differences are harmonised by the Spirit and charity becomes authentic in accepting one another. So the experience of migration can be the announcement of the paschal mystery, in which death and resurrection make for the creation of a new humanity in which there is no longer slave or foreigner (Galatians 3:28).

Lord Jesus Christ,
you told us that the one who asks will receive,
the one who seeks will find,
the one who knocks will have the door opened.
Grant us an understanding of your commands
and the strength to act upon them,
help us to treat others as we would like them to treat us,
for that is the meaning of the Law and the Prophets.
Amen.

Adapted from Matthew 7:7,12

Pavel ended up sleeping in a squat for a period of time. Fortunately, one day, Pavel heard about the Cardinal Hume Centre, where, on arrival he was offered food and refreshment, a shower, a laundry service and advice. Pavel got clothing from the Centre's Charity shop and was linked with Westminster City Council and the police enabling him to get replacement ID papers. Pavel was referred to the Centre's ESOL (English as a Second or Other Language) service to help him to improve his English language skills. Soon after Pavel found a job working as a kitchen porter.

Pavel, 21, Polish man taken from *The Ground of Justice*

My two Italian flatmates who arrived recently had a real nightmare trying to open a bank account. They had to arrange a number of letters, go back and forth, and the whole thing was really complicated. As there are so many things newly arriving people do not know, maybe the parish could gather expertise and knowledge of its members. For example, if a migrant wants to get a teaching job, maybe the church could say 'ring parishioner X who has the expertise and who will provide you with the necessary information'. The same thing with writing a CV – the CV I wrote in Italy would have been totally useless for finding a job in Britain. It's a cultural thing. So, maybe the church could help migrants drawing on help of the parishioners.

Italian woman taken from *The Ground of Justice*

Lord Jesus Christ,
you told us that the one who asks will receive,
the one who seeks will find,
the one who knocks will have the door opened.
Grant us an understanding of your commands
and the strength to act upon them,
help us to treat others as we would like them to treat us,
for that is the meaning of the Law and the Prophets.
Amen.

Adapted from Matthew 7:7,12

'Unbind him, let him go free'

Having raised Lazarus from the dead, Jesus commanded the bystanders to 'unbind him' and 'let him go free'. Far from leaving others free, the temptation each of us faces is that of setting conditions to our giving and expecting returns on our generosity. Leaving somebody free is an integral part of respecting their dignity and integrity. Helping another doesn't mean imposing solutions, it means listening and responding to what they have to say.

From Pope John Paul II's message on World Migration Day 1999

6. The parish, a house where the guest feels at ease, welcomes all and discriminates against none, for no one there is an outsider. It combines the stability and security people feel in their own home with the movement or transience of those who are passing through. Wherever there is a living sense of parish, differences between locals and strangers fade or disappear in the overriding awareness that all belong to God the one Father.

The importance of the parish in welcoming the stranger, in integrating baptised persons from different cultures and in dialoguing with believers of other religions stems from the mission of every parish community and its significance within society. This is not an optional, supplementary role for the parish community, but a duty inherent in its task as an institution.

Lord Jesus Christ,
you told us that the one who asks will receive,
the one who seeks will find,
the one who knocks will have the door opened.
Grant us an understanding of your commands
and the strength to act upon them,
help us to treat others as we would like them to treat us,
for that is the meaning of the Law and the Prophets.
Amen.

Adapted from Matthew 7:7,12

When they were near Jerusalem and had come in sight of Bethphage on the Mount of Olives, Jesus sent two disciples, saying to them, 'Go to the village facing you, and you will immediately find a tethered donkey and a colt with her. Untie them and bring them to me. If anyone says anything to you, you are to say, "The Master needs them and will send them back directly." ' This took place to fulfil the prophecy:

Say to the daughter of Zion:
Look, your king comes to you;
he is humble, he rides on a donkey
and on a colt, the foal of a beast of burden.

So the disciples went out and did as Jesus had told them. They brought the donkey and the colt, then they laid their cloaks on their backs and he sat on them. Great crowds of people spread their cloaks on the road, while others were cutting branches from the trees and spreading them in his path. The crowds who went in front of him and those who followed were all shouting:

'Hosanna to the Son of David!
Blessings on him who comes in the name of the Lord!
Hosanna in the highest heavens!'

And when he entered Jerusalem, the whole city was in turmoil. 'Who is this?' people asked, and the crowds answered, 'This is the prophet Jesus from Nazareth in Galilee.'

Matthew 21: 1-11

Have I managed to recognise Christ in others? Or has my acclamation, my 'Hosanna' on Sunday been quickly forgotten amid the turmoil and troubles of daily life?

Lord Jesus Christ,
you told us that the one who asks will receive,
the one who seeks will find,
the one who knocks will have the door opened.
Grant us an understanding of your commands
and the strength to act upon them,
help us to treat others as we would like them to treat us,
for that is the meaning of the Law and the Prophets.
Amen.

Adapted from Matthew 7:7,12

Opening Prayer

Leader:
May God be gracious to us and bless us
and make his face to shine upon us,
that your way may be known upon earth,
your saving power among all nations.

Group:
**Let the peoples praise you, O God;
let all the peoples praise you.**

Leader:
Let the nations be glad and sing for joy,
for you judge the peoples with equity
and guide the nations upon earth.

Group:
**Let the peoples praise you, O God;
let all the peoples praise you.**

Leader:
The earth has yielded its increase;
God, our God, has blessed us.

Group:
**May God continue to bless us;
let all the ends of the earth revere him.**

From Psalm 67

All:
Glory be to the Father...

Leader:
Lord, in this moment of silence
help us to be still
so that your word may enter our minds,
touch our hearts,
and direct our lives to you.

After a short silence the group or an individual says:

Gracious and holy Father,
give us wisdom to perceive you,
intelligence to understand you,
diligence to seek you,
patience to wait for you,
eyes to behold you,
a heart to meditate on you,
and a life to proclaim you;
through the power of the
Spirit of Jesus Christ our Lord,
Amen.

St. Benedict of Nursia (c.480-c.547

From the Sunday Scriptures – Palm Sunday (Matthew 21: 1-11)

When they were near Jerusalem and had come in sight of Bethphage on the Mount of Olives, Jesus sent two disciples, saying to them, 'Go to the village facing you, and you will immediately find a tethered donkey and a colt with her. Untie them and bring them to me. If anyone says anything to you, you are to say, "The Master needs them and will send them back directly." ' This took place to fulfil the prophecy:

Say to the daughter of Zion:
Look, your king comes to you;
he is humble, he rides on a donkey
and on a colt, the foal of a beast of burden.

So the disciples went out and did as Jesus had told them. They brought the donkey and the colt, then they laid their cloaks on their backs and he sat on them. Great crowds of people spread their cloaks on the road, while others were cutting branches from the trees and spreading them in his path. The crowds who went in front of him and those who followed were all shouting:

'Hosanna to the Son of David!
Blessings on him who comes in the name of the Lord!
Hosanna in the highest heavens!'

And when he entered Jerusalem, the whole city was in turmoil. 'Who is this?' people asked, and the crowds answered, 'This is the prophet Jesus from Nazareth in Galilee.'

Following a short period of silence you may wish to share an image, a thought, a phrase, a question that has struck you.

For Reflection

Over the last six weeks we have asked ourselves a straightforward question. Who is my neighbour? More particularly, we have reflected on the quality of welcome newcomers receive from us and the parishes we are a part of, asking ourselves whether or not we have taken the trouble to discover something of their story, address their needs, recognise their giftedness, be reshaped by their presence. Our natural inclination may be to keep a 'safe' distance from those we do not know; but the dignity conferred on us at baptism challenges us to reach out to our neighbours, baptised and unbaptised. The former is already a brother or sister in Christ, whilst all have a right to that fulfilment and flourishing which stems from knowing God (Father, Son and Spirit) in whose image all have been created.

This Holy Week the person, the neighbour, we are called to keep company with is Christ. That first Palm Sunday he was welcomed enthusiastically, with huge gestures and plenty of noise. And yet, in a short while, the crowds would turn on him. How firm is your resolution to keep faith with this migrant, whose kingdom, was not of this world?

Having celebrated Palm Sunday will you stay awake in the garden on Maundy Thursday? On Good Friday will you spend time at the foot of the Cross? On Easter Sunday will you rush to celebrate his resurrection, much as his disciples rushed to the empty tomb? In spending time with him will you take the trouble to hear what he has to say: his command to celebrate the Eucharist 'in memory of me', his call to serve as he has served, the challenge to put away the sword, his declaration of thirst?

Will the pattern of his life reshape the pattern of yours? Will his obedience to the Father challenge you to build the Father's Kingdom and not your own? Will his resurrection colour your approach to suffering and death? When faced with your failures, will you allow the forgiveness he won for us, to help you begin again?

Share your thoughts on this reflection. How does this week's Scripture reading and reflection encourage you? Where are you affirmed? Where are you challenged? What impact might this have on your daily living?

From Erga migrantes caritas Christi

15. In the foreigner a Christian sees not simply a neighbour, but the face of Christ Himself, who was born in a manger and fled into Egypt, where he was a foreigner, summing up and repeating in His own life the basic experience of His people (cf. Matthew 2:13ff). Born away from home and coming from another land (cf. Luke 2:4-7), 'he came to dwell among us' (cf. John 1:11,14) and spent His public life on the move, going through towns and villages (cf. Luke 13:22; Matthew 9:35). After His resurrection, still a foreigner and unknown, He appeared on the way to Emmaus to two of His disciples, who only recognised Him at the breaking of the bread (cf. Luke 24:35). So Christians are followers of a man on the move 'who has nowhere to lay his head (Matthew 8:20; Luke 9:58)'.

Leader: Aloud or in the silence of our hearts let us bring to the Father our thanks (pause)…

Leader: In sorrow let us ask the Father for forgiveness (pause)…

Leader: With confidence let us entrust to the Father our cares and concerns (pause)…

Closing prayer

Lord, forgive us the times we have ignored those in need,
or refused a welcome to those you have embraced.
Strengthen us with your grace, open our hearts,
that our thoughts, words and deeds,
may reflect your love for the neighbours you set before us,
for you live and reign with the Father and the Holy Spirit,
one God, for ever and ever.
Amen.

Who is My Neighbour?

Christ, my neighbour, is the way.
Christ, my neighbour, is the truth.
Christ, my neighbour, is the life.
To him be glory and praise for ever and ever.
Amen.

Read the Scripture from the Palm Sunday - Matthew 21: 1-11

The version used at Mass can be found at the beginning of the Group Session for Week Five (pp.84-85). You may, of course, read from your own Bible.

Background

The Palm Sunday Gospel according to Matthew ought to be compared to the earlier version in Mark (11:1-10). For Matthew, Jesus' arrival at Jerusalem is narrated with the greatest solemnity as it represents the arrival of the Messianic King (Matthew 1:1, 1:17) into the holy city of David (2 Samuel 5:6-10), Jerusalem. This entry marks also the arrival of the long-expected prophet illustrated by the fact that Jesus' entry fulfils new prophecies for Isaiah (62:11) and Zechariah (9:9). The arrival of the prophetic Messiah is, however, the moment for the judgement of Israel: 'the daughter of Zion' as the Bride of God (Isaiah 62:11) experiences the moment of salvation but rejects it by later condemning Jesus (Matthew 27:25). To those who believed in Jesus, however, his entry was a moment of salvation. The ancient Hebrew form is retained through the Hosanna acclamation (Matthew 21:9). With this acclamation it is confirmed that in Jesus, God is truly with us (Matthew 1:23).

O my God,
with my whole heart, in spite of my heart,
do I receive this cross I feared so much!
Nor for anything in the world
would I wish that it had not come, since You willed it.
I keep it with gratitude and with joy,
as I do everything that comes from Your hand;
and I shall strive to carry it without letting it drag,
with all the respect and all the affection
which Your works deserve.
Amen.

St. Francis De Sales (1567-1622)

a tethered donkey.... a beast of burden

Have you ever stopped to think of about the animals represented in the crib? Off hand, one may think they are there simply to remind us that it was a stable, yet the lowly donkey figures again and again in Christ's life. Besides being there at his birth, shortly thereafter, this beast of burden accompanied the Holy Family on their flight from their homeland to Egypt. While this journey effectively initiated Christ's earthly life as a migrant, the donkey is there again for that final trip into Jerusalem and into the hands of his captors.

Like the parables and most other biblical passages, the symbolism and foreshadowing may not be readily apparent. Moreover, connections with our own life may take more than a quick glance. On that last journey to Jerusalem, the humble Christ was himself burdened with our sins that he carried to the Cross to forge for each of us a way to the Father. Perhaps we too are burdened - by our desire for material goods and other earthly goals that tether each of us and thus prevent us from reaching out to our neighbour.

O my God,
with my whole heart, in spite of my heart,
do I receive this cross I feared so much!
Nor for anything in the world
would I wish that it had not come, since You willed it.
I keep it with gratitude and with joy,
as I do everything that comes from Your hand;
and I shall strive to carry it without letting it drag,
with all the respect and all the affection
which Your works deserve.
Amen.

St. Francis De Sales (1567-1622)

Hosanna, Son of David

The waving of palm fronds and the cry 'Hosanna' was a traditional Jewish practice. It looked forward to the promised redemption. A cry of both praise and petition the word Hosanna literally means 'save us'. 'Hosanna' has been a part of the Christian liturgical vocabulary for centuries. This Palm Sunday it will have enriched the liturgy commemorating Christ's entry into Jerusalem. In addressing this cry to Jesus, and referring to King David, the crowds who went in front of him, as well as those who followed him, were making a clear connection between the promised Messiah and the person of Jesus. He was to be their Saviour.

In the Church, people of many different cultures are gathered together in Christ, 'the one human family in which God has made his dwelling' (Revelation 21:3). Just as the early Christians incorporated Jewish traditions, we are asked to recognise the gifts and cultural traditions that our neighbours bring with them. These too can enrich our communities and our celebration of the Liturgy.

O my God,
with my whole heart, in spite of my heart,
do I receive this cross I feared so much!
Nor for anything in the world
would I wish that it had not come, since You willed it.
I keep it with gratitude and with joy,
as I do everything that comes from Your hand;
and I shall strive to carry it without letting it drag,
with all the respect and all the affection
which Your works deserve.
Amen.

St. Francis De Sales (1567-162?)

Who is this?

In his book, *Truth and Tolerance*, Pope Benedict XVI states that 'Faith is no private path to God'. In other words, faith implies a shared journey to the Father.

The faith given to each of us at our baptism unites us as brothers and sisters in Christ - to walk together in his footsteps. It is clear from the Holy Scriptures that Christ spent a great deal of time listening to those that he met as he travelled the lands of Israel. He showed us that only by coming to know and respect another's background can we begin to build communion. It is only with true feelings for another, when we have taken the time to listen, understand and see beyond the surface, that we will see Christ in that person. It is only then that we can begin to proclaim the Good News. We too should ask 'Who is this?'

From Pope John Paul II's message on World Migration Day 1998
3. For the believer, accepting others is not only philanthropy or a natural concern for his fellow man. It is far more, because in every human being he knows he is meeting Christ.

O my God,
with my whole heart, in spite of my heart,
do I receive this cross I feared so much!
Nor for anything in the world
would I wish that it had not come, since You willed it.
I keep it with gratitude and with joy,
as I do everything that comes from Your hand;
and I shall strive to carry it without letting it drag,
with all the respect and all the affection
which Your works deserve.
Amen.

St. Francis De Sales (1567-1622)

Such as my love has been for you, so must your love be for each other
                                                                    John 13:3

While public foot washing may no longer be the norm, in ancient civilizations and certainly, in the time of Jesus, sandals were the main form of footwear. Therefore the history recounted in the Old Testament makes mention of water being provided for guests and visitors to wash their dirty and weary feet (Genesis 18:4 and 19:2, see also Luke 7:44 amd 1 Tim 5:10).

According to St. John, Jesus washed the feet of the Apostles gathered around him at the Last Supper (John 13:2-15). Yet Christ's washing of his apostles' feet was so much more than an everyday action. Note, Peter's reluctance to have Christ do this for him. In the Upper Room what was an every day practice became sacramental – that is a visible action that to leads us to ponder our faith more deeply. With total humility, Christ, the Master or Teacher bent down to wash the feet of his disciples. Not only did he preach the message of love; he put it into action. Service underpinned Our Lord's earthly ministry. On Holy Thursday he challenges us to do the same, 'such as my love has been for you, so must your love be for each other'. Setting aside pride and self-centredness we are called to attend to our fellow human beings; not just our brothers and sisters in faith, but all who have been created in God's image.

O my God,
with my whole heart, in spite of my heart,
do I receive this cross I feared so much!
Nor for anything in the world
would I wish that it had not come, since You willed it.
I keep it with gratitude and with joy,
as I do everything that comes from Your hand;
and I shall strive to carry it without letting it drag,
with all the respect and all the affection
which Your works deserve.
Amen.

                                          St. Francis De Sales (1567-1622)

a man from Cyrene, Simon by name, and enlisted him to carry his cross
Matthew 27:32

On this most solemn of days, we walk with heavy hearts accompanying Christ as he endures the pain of our sins – a pain inflicted by his captors on our behalf. When the pain and weight of the Cross were more than his human body could withstand, the Romans soldiers commanded a bystander to help him. Who was this man that was pressed into service to help carry the Cross? While little is known of Simon of Cyrene, we do know that he was visiting Jerusalem after having travelled a great distance. Cyrene was a colony founded by the Greeks on the coast of North Africa – near present day Tripoli, Libya. It is likely that Simon had saved for some time in order to make this trip to Jerusalem to celebrate Passover. Although Simon had little choice but to help Jesus, how often do we reflect on that moment, wishing we could lighten Christ's load?

Today, as we look around our parishes, how many of us are far from 'home', having travelled significant distances? How many of us would have incurred significant personal costs, not just financial but separation from family and friends as well, to make a life here? Like Simon of Cyrene, we too are chosen. Regardless of circumstances, each of us are called to lighten the load of others sharing the message of Christ imprinted on our hearts and minds at baptism. At tomorrow's Easter Vigil, we will be invited to recite the Creed and to renew our baptismal promises. Let us live as one human family. Let us deepen the bonds of unity. Strengthened by grace and grounded in faith, let us transcend the barriers we perpetuate.

From Pope John Paul II's message on World Migration Day 2003

2. Membership in the Catholic community is not determined by nationality, or by social or ethnic origin, but essentially by faith in Jesus Christ and Baptism in the name of the Holy Trinity.

O my God,
with my whole heart, in spite of my heart,
do I receive this cross I feared so much!
Nor for anything in the world
would I wish that it had not come, since You willed it.
I keep it with gratitude and with joy,
as I do everything that comes from Your hand;
and I shall strive to carry it without letting it drag,
with all the respect and all the affection
which Your works deserve.
Amen.

St. Francis De Sales (1567-1622)

It was very early on the first day of the week and still dark, when Mary of Magdala came to the tomb. She saw that the stone had been moved away from the tomb and came running to Simon Peter and the other disciple, the one Jesus loved. 'They have taken the Lord out of the tomb,' she said 'and we don't know where they have put him.' So Peter set out with the other disciples to go to the tomb. They ran together, but the other disciple, running faster than Peter, reached the tomb first; he bent down and saw the linen cloths lying on the ground, but did not go in. Simon Peter who was following now came up, went right into the tomb, saw the linen cloths on the ground, and also the cloth that had been over his head; this was not with the linen cloths but rolled up in a place by itself. Then the other disciple who had reached the tomb first also went in; he saw and he believed. Till this moment they had failed to understand the teaching of Scripture, that he must rise from the dead.

John 20: 1-9

In this gospel passage we are told that the Apostles came to understand the teaching of Scripture. What have you learnt this Lent? What resolutions have you made, that your welcoming of others might be sincere and your reaching out to your neighbour be a proclamation of the Risen Lord?

Alleluia, sing to Jesus,
his the sceptre, his the throne
alleluia, his the triumph,
his the victory alone:
hark! the songs of peaceful Sion
thunder like a mighty flood;
Jesus out of ev'ry nation,
hath redeemed us by his blood.

W. Chatterton Dix (1837-98)

Notes